Cool Kid Musicians

Laura Hamilton Waxman

Lerner Publications • Minneapolis

For Yana, my guitar-playing, song-singing girl
—L.H.W.

Copyright © 2020 by Lerner Publishing Group, Inc.

All rights reserved. International copyright secured. No part of this book may be reproduced, stored in a retrieval system, or transmitted in any form or by any means—electronic, mechanical, photocopying, recording, or otherwise—without the prior written permission of Lerner Publishing Group, Inc., except for the inclusion of brief quotations in an acknowledged review.

Lerner Publications Company
An imprint of Lerner Publishing Group, Inc.
241 First Avenue North
Minneapolis, MN 55401 USA

For reading levels and more information, look up this title at www.lernerbooks.com.

Library of Congress Cataloging-in-Publication Data

Names: Waxman, Laura Hamilton, author.
Title: Cool kid musicians / Laura Hamilton Waxman.
Description: Minneapolis : Lerner Publications, 2020. | Series: Lightning bolt books—Kids in charge! | Audience: Grades K-3. | Includes bibliographical references and index.
Identifiers: LCCN 2019016951 (print) | LCCN 2019017242 (ebook) | ISBN 9781541583221 (eb pdf) | ISBN 9781541577046 (lb : alk. paper) | ISBN 9781541589131 (pb : alk. paper)
Subjects: LCSH: Child musicians—Juvenile literature.
Classification: LCC ML3929 (ebook) | LCC ML3929 .W39 2020 (print) | DDC 780.23—dc23

LC record available at https://lccn.loc.gov/2019016951

Manufactured in the United States of America
1-46726-47717-8/12/2019

Table of Contents

Awesome Musicians — 4

Pop and Rap — 6

Rock and Roll — 10

Cool Jazz — 14

Classical — 16

You Can Do It! — 20

Did You Know? — 21

Glossary — 22

Further Reading — 23

Index — 24

Awesome Musicians

Some kids are born to sing, drum, or strum. They love to make music and share it with others.

These kids know how to put on a show. They thrill their audiences with beautiful and exciting music. They have won many fans with their talents.

Pop and Rap

Have you ever wanted to sing your heart out for millions of people? These kids have, and they made their dreams come true.

Angelica Hale

Angelica Hale was nine when she competed on *America's Got Talent*. Her singing wowed the show's judges, and she won second place.

Angelica returned to *America's Got Talent* for the 2019 champion season.

Sparsh Shah

Sparsh Shah is a rapper and singer. He writes his own music and wrote his first song at six years old.

Sparsh has performed his music for more than 125 audiences.

Sparsh starred in a movie about his life.

Sparsh uses a wheelchair. He has an illness that makes his bones very weak. Sparsh has performed on TV and on stages around the world.

Rock and Roll

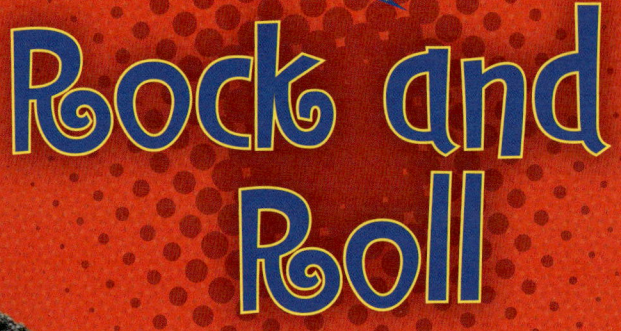

Do you like to rock out to your favorite music? These kids know how to jam!

School of Rock is about a substitute teacher that forms a rock band with his students.

Eamonn Hubert

Eamonn Hubert plays electric guitar. He plays in a band with his dad. He has also performed across the country in a musical called *School of Rock*.

Avery Molek

Avery Molek is a drumming superstar. Millions of people have watched his videos on YouTube. He has played with some famous musicians too.

Kiss is Avery's favorite band, and he played with them at one of their concerts.

Yoyoka Soma

Yoyoka Soma started playing drums when she was two years old. She has performed on more than one hundred stages. Her dream is to become the best drummer in the world.

Famous singer Robert Plant was amazed by Yoyoka's skill.

Cool Jazz

Joey Alexander

Joey Alexander is a popular jazz pianist. He has already recorded four albums. Two of them were nominated for a Grammy Award.

Joey taught himself to play piano at the age of six.

Sophie impressed *America's Got Talent* judge Howie Mandel.

Sophie Fatu

Sophie Fatu is a little kid with a big voice. Thousands of people watch her videos on YouTube. She has also performed on *America's Got Talent*.

Classical

Some kids fall in love with classical music. They love the rich sound of bows on strings.

Alma Deutscher

Alma is a talented pianist and violinist. She writes music too. She composed her first opera when she was seven years old.

Alma performs around the world.

Justin Yu

Justin loves to play cello. He performs with a group of kids called the Joyous String Ensemble.

Justin was three when he started playing the cello.

Kids like Alma and Justin are successful. They're fun to watch and listen to. They put all they've got into the music that they love.

You Can Do It!

Do you want to be a musician? First, you have to choose an instrument. Maybe your instrument is your singing voice. You might need to try out a few instruments before you decide what you like. The next step is to learn how to play. Many kids take lessons from a music teacher. But some kids teach themselves. It's also important to practice. The more you practice, the better you'll be. Soon you'll be ready to perform!

Did You Know?

- Angelica Hale was the youngest person to win second place on *America's Got Talent*.

- Eamonn Hubert's main instrument is the guitar. But he also knows how to play eight other instruments!

- Alma Deutscher's most famous opera is *Cinderella*. She finished it when she was twelve.

Glossary

album: a musical recording with songs on it

classical music: a type of music that began in Europe hundreds of years ago. Classical music includes opera and symphony.

compose: to write music

Grammy Award: one of the most famous awards a musician can win

jazz: a type of music invented by African Americans near the end of the nineteenth century

nominate: to choose someone for an award

opera: a kind of classical music that tells a story with singing and instruments

talent: a special ability to do something, such as play music or sing

Further Reading

Alma Deutscher
https://www.almadeutscher.com

Anderson, Michelle. *In a Band*. Vero Beach, FL: Rourke, 2019.

Angelica Hale
https://angelicahale.com

Avery Molek
http://averydrummer.com

Haynes, Norma Jean. *Make Music! A Kid's Guide to Creating Rhythm, Playing with Sound, and Conducting and Composing Music*. North Adams, MA: Storey, 2019.

Joey Alexander
http://joeyalexandermusic.com

Waxman, Laura Hamilton. *Cool Kid Online Stars*. Minneapolis: Lerner Publications, 2020.

Index

album, 14

band, 11

classical, 16

jazz, 14

opera, 17

song, 8

Photo Acknowledgments

Image credits: AlexMaster/Shutterstock.com, p. 2; sturti/Getty Images, p. 4; Yuri_Arcurs/Getty Images, p. 5; Fresh Meat Media LLC/Getty Images, p. 6; AP Photo/WENNR, p. 7; Mireya Acierto/Getty Images, p. 8; Lukas Gojda Shutterstock.com, p. 9; Thomas Northcut/Getty Images, p. 10; John Phillips/Getty Images, p. 11; Brill/ullstein bild/Getty Images, p. 12; Taylor Hill/Getty Images, p. 13; PASCAL PAVANI/AFP/Getty Images, p. 14; Presley Ann/FilmMagic/Getty Images, p. 15; sumire8/Shutterstock.com, p. 16; Michael Gruber/Life Ball 2017/Getty Images, p. 17; Mindscape studio/Shutterstock.com, p. 18; Adam Sorenson/Barcroft Image/Barcroft Media via/Getty Images, p. 19; Maksym Bondarchuk/Shutterstock.com, p. 21; Vector pack/Shutterstock.com, p. 22.

Cover: Paul Zimmerman/WireImage for The Recording Academy/Getty Images.

Main body text set in Billy Infant regular. Typeface provided by SparkType.